Wingers and Leapers and Creepers – a world of fantastical insects

Wingers and Leapers and Creepers – a world of fantastical insects

Michael Glover and Ruth Dupré

Wingers and Leapers and Creepers –
a world of fantastical insects

Copyright © Michael Glover and Ruth Dupré 2021

The moral rights of the author and artist have been asserted.

Cover image © Ruth Dupré

Cover Font: *Disgusting Behaviour*. Thanks to Eduardo Recife / Misprinted Type ©
[http://www.misprintedtype.com]

ISBN 978-1-915045-06-5

www.1889books

A Note

This book of poems and monoprints represents an attempt to capture a very particular moment – a slow, sun-struck summer's day (or perhaps it is a few such days, all blurred into one) – in the small country kitchen of a house in the Charente Maritime in the middle of France.

The windows were flung open wide – it was hotter than hot – and the door to the short flight of steep stone steps that took you down into the garden, thrown back. And it was then that they began to drift in, quite inconsequentially, it seemed, at first: tiny armies of wingers and leapers and creepers. The flies and the dragonflies. The wasps and the blundering bee. The butterfly and the mosquito. All in pursuit of somewhere to go for a while. They were everywhere, but they were not much of a bother because most of them were so small and so intent upon what they themselves were up to – which had nothing to do with us.

As we stared at them, we began to see a rich comedy in their routines – some seemed to be the equivalent of plate-dropping clowns, others jet-plane pilots with a furious mission. Ruth decided to set them down on a paper delicate enough to record the precise nature of their different characters, a Japanese paper light and flimsy and fragile enough to mimic the no-sooner-there-than-gone lives of this superabundance of wingers and leapers and creepers.

As she drew them, their persons, their characters began to merge and to blur somewhat, becoming a gorgeous array of hybrid beings, part dragonfly, part fly, part wasp, part mosquito. Life had become even more uproarious than ever.

And then, a year later or so, I looked back and took renewed delight in what she had done, and a cycle of poems emerged as if in response, or perhaps by way of a conclusion.

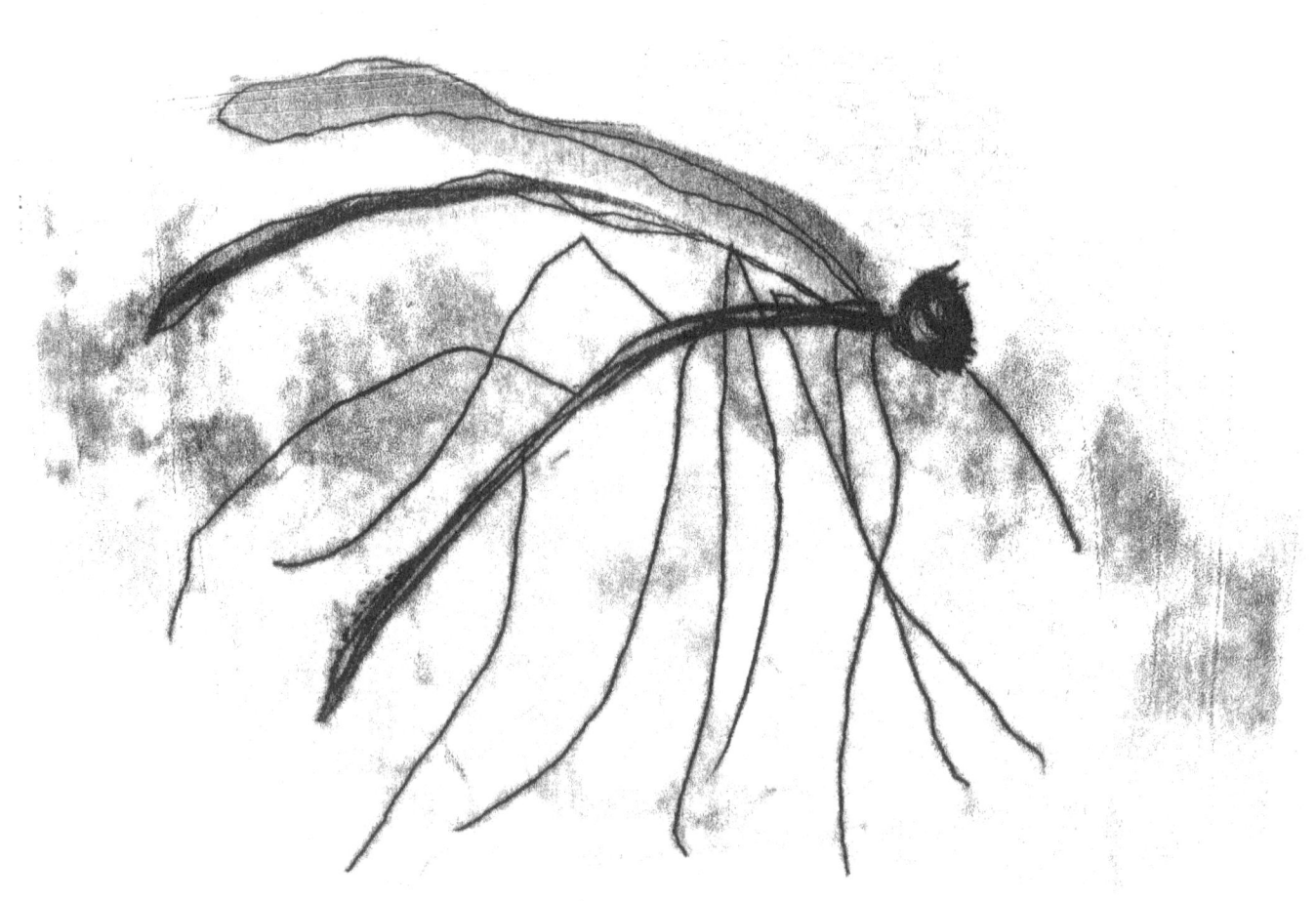

The Warning

It descends, with a sudden sideways zip,
From ceiling height,
Onto this table top,
Ready to warn, ready to challenge...

Don't swivel the bulbous blank discs
Of your eyes towards me so strangely,
You man of war you.

Don't jiggle and dangle
The thinness of your filament legs
By way of warning.

I know you for what you are.
You are too tiny to be truly menacing.

Onward I Go

My knot-black head, tough as a tiny nut,
With its jiggling twin antennae,
Will keep me going.

It knows that all the drama of my short life
Lies directly in front of me
Like a huge explosion.

It is no easy matter, I tell you,
To be walking,
Alternating as we go,
On all six legs
With the hesitant delicacy
Of the ballerina's tread.

And yet I must keep moving
Because I will be
On the wide world's stage,
To the applause of thousand upon thousand,
Before the moon has risen.

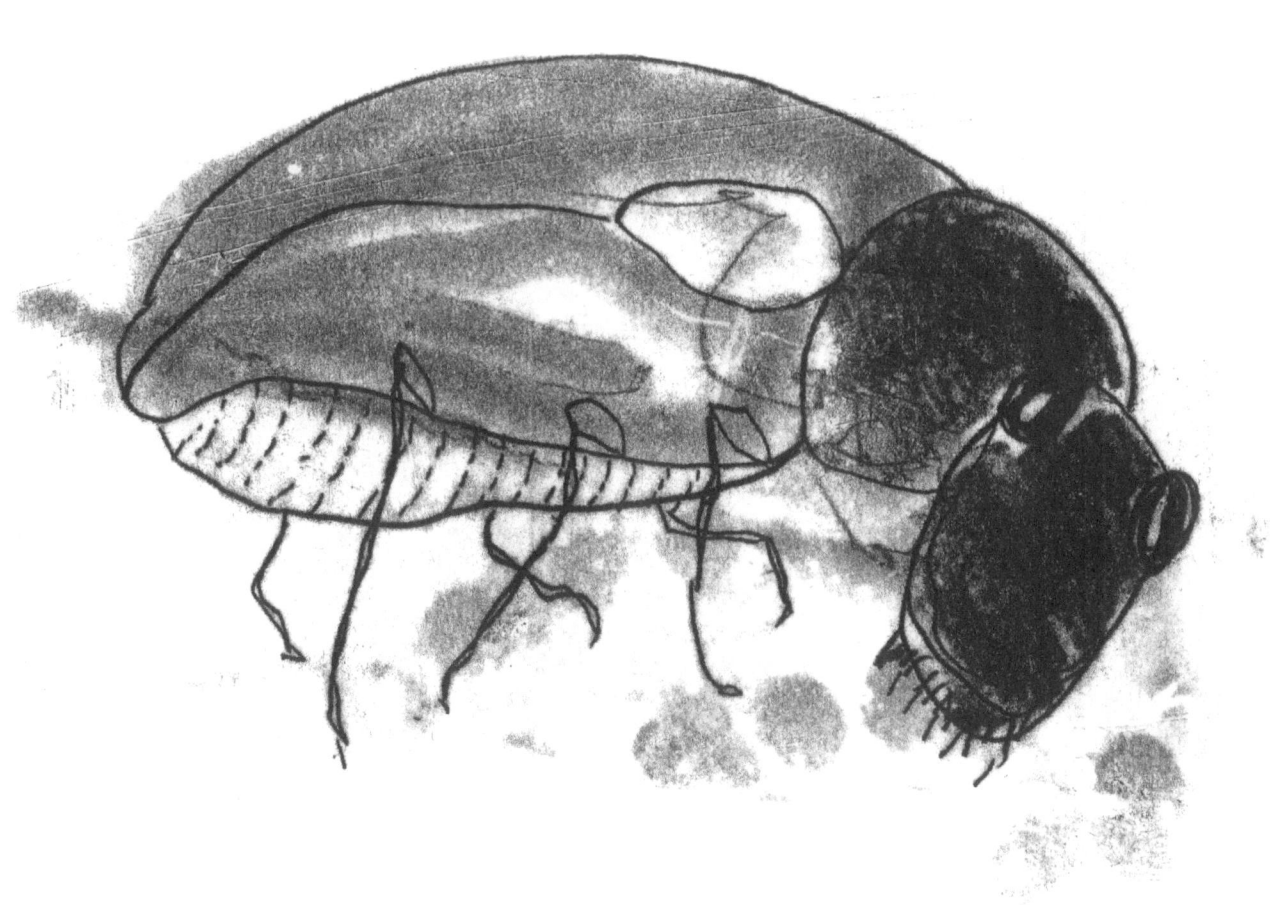

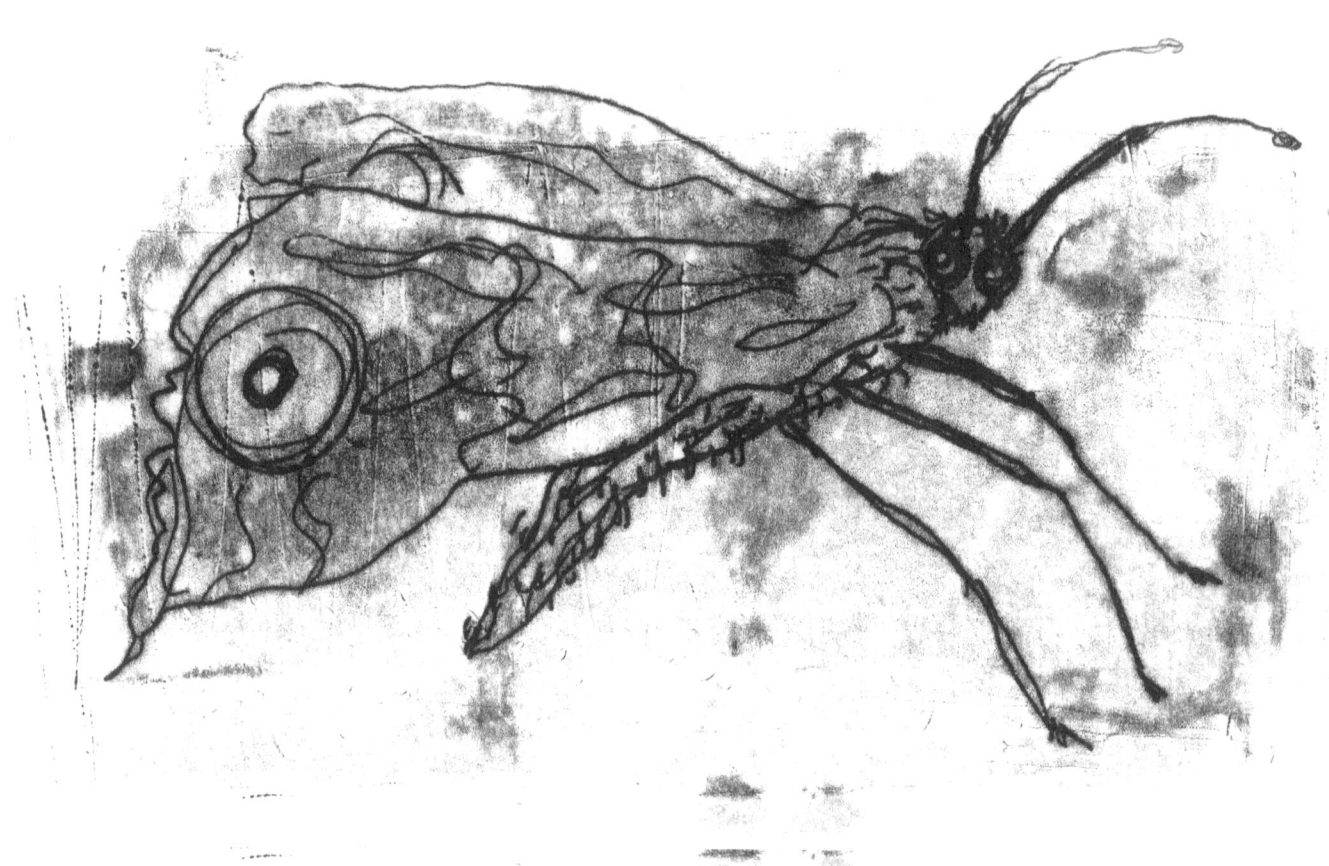

Emerging from the Chrysalis

Was it the beginning of something,
When I emerged
From being so crisp and tight curled
Into this –
A flourish, a wondrous flap of frippery –
Wings or bed sheets perhaps –
Out here in the world?

If you could tell me who I am,
Describe to me exactly how I relate to you,
Down there in your chair,
With your book and your sideways fidgets,
I could easily let you know how much
We should fear each other,
You monster you.

Passing Through

I have this strange idea
That you are staring at me
In this corner here

Because you fear me more
Than the onset of darkness
Or that odd, sulphurous stink in the air.

Let me tell you something then.
I am just passing through.
I care nothing for you.

An Exchange of Glances

When I look back at you
Through my curious black saucer eyes,
I ask myself: Who are you?
And why exactly are you here in my world?

You sit there in your chair,
Pretending to be at rest
With your brimming glass
And that newspaper furled in your lap,
But I know that in a second
You could leap up
And deal me a blow
That would despatch me
To the next world.

You care nothing for my beauty.
You care nothing for the flourish
Of these wings of mine
Which, when even at rest,
Seem to hint at their gorgeousness
In full glorious flight.

In this passing moment,
When we are doing nothing but
Look at each other, back and forth,
Me to you, you to me,
I ask you once again,
In fact I plead with you:
Why not try to understand me
Or, at worst, leave me be?
I am no threat to your world.
You simply do not understand me.

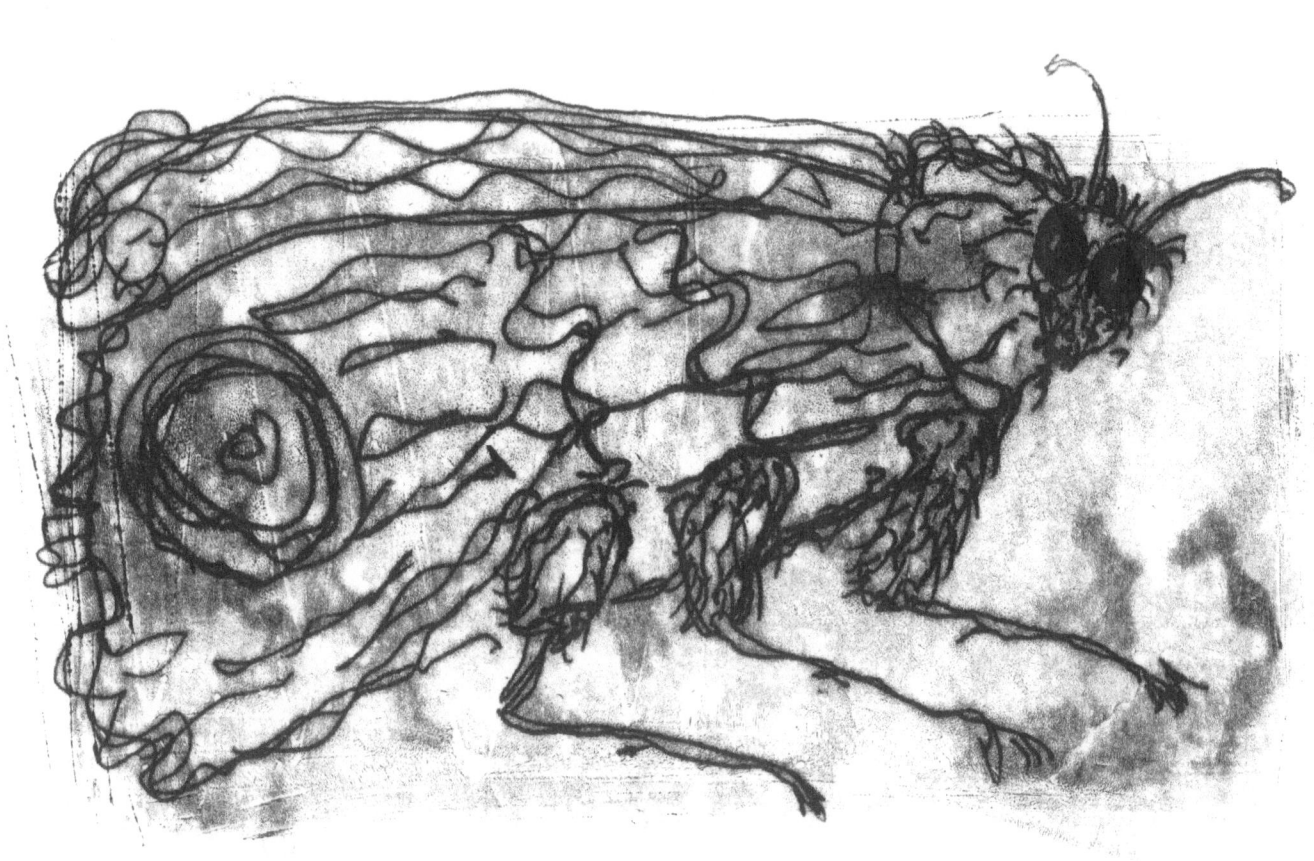

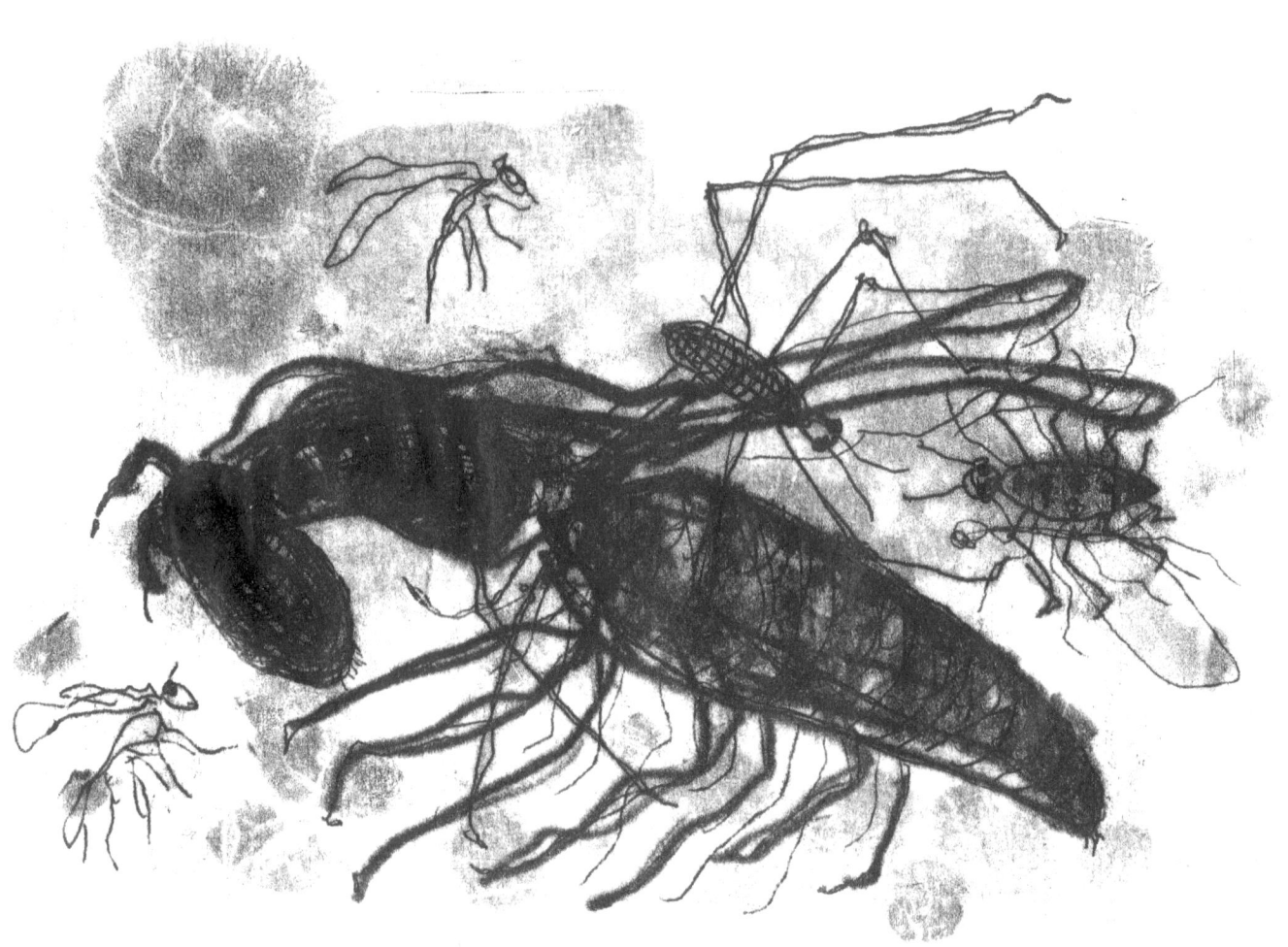

Wind-Lifted

When in the air like this,
Blurrily wind-lifted,
Suspended between here and there,
It is all about balance
And acute alertness.

I know what there is to be done.
It is as simple as blinking awake
Into the light of new morning.

I am to be carried to that window ledge,
Where I will settle for a little while,
Until such time as I
Lift off again,
With a tiny flourish.

It is all about bearing,
With so little care,
My pin-light, dust-mote-light self
Through the air...

See how I do it now.
Marvel at my acrobatics
As I go somewhere.

Never insult me by calling me
Ungainly or awkward.

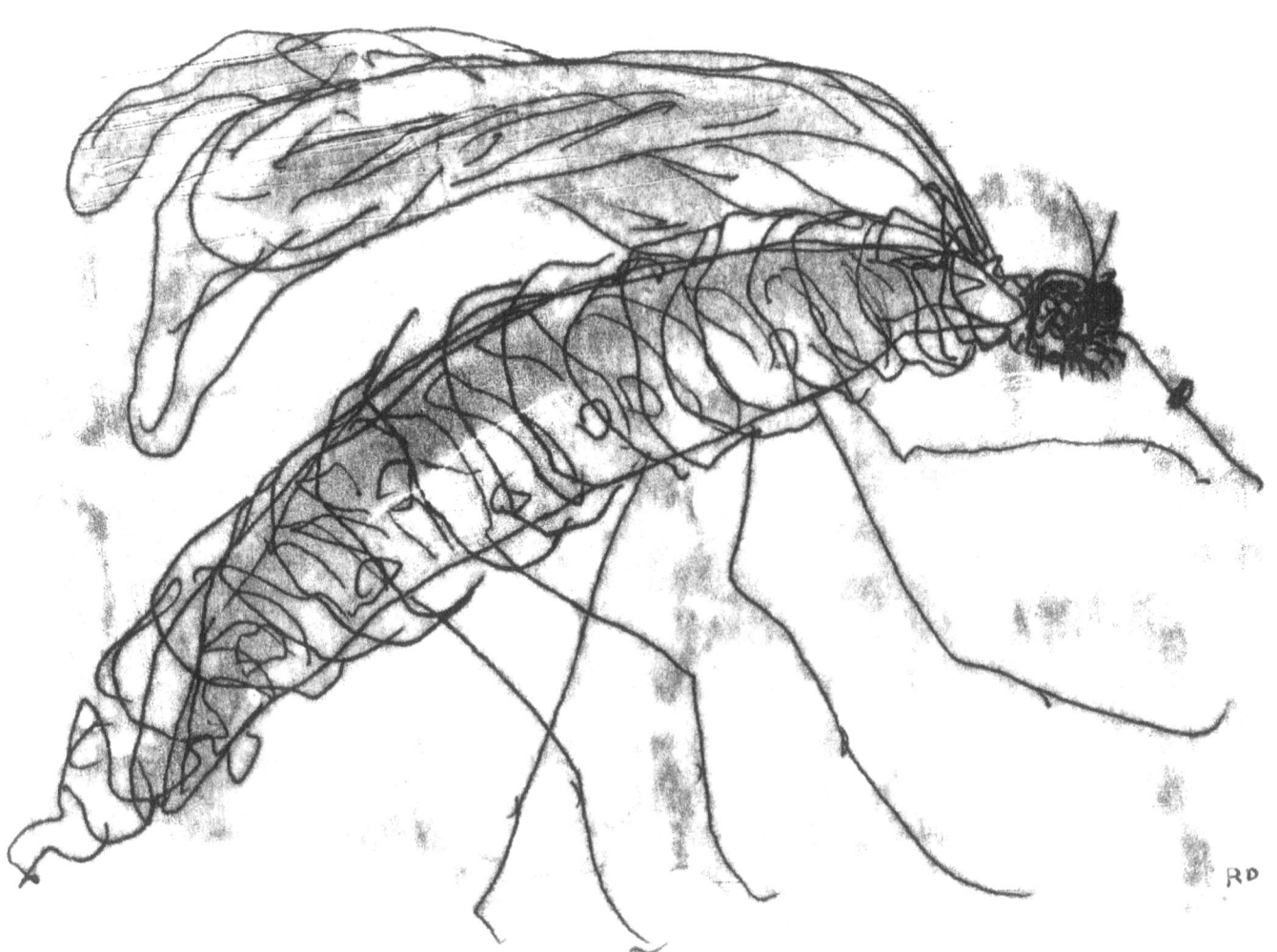

In Disguise

Left me hide myself here
As if I am one of a threesome,
One member perhaps
Of this docile plant kingdom
Set in a tidy garden.

No one will see me
If I stay perfectly still
And stop – as far as I can –
The wind teasing out
My spread of gossamer-light wings.

That is the difficult part, of course –
To keep my wings fast to my sides
In good quiet order,
That and these strange
Double antennae of mine –
How I wish they would droop a little more!
Which protect me, I pray,
From all worldly dangers
Here and hereafter.

What I am Not

Do not call me
What I am not –
A hippopotamus perhaps
Or something equally drooped, slow and heavy.

Do not insult me by mouthing off with:
That creature is too clumsy
To walk, to fly, or even to hop.

In fact, it can barely turn its head
To say a yawny goodbye
As it slithers or drags itself off.

You know nothing of my speed
Or my agility.
You have never seen me leave,
In a gulp of the breath – like this!

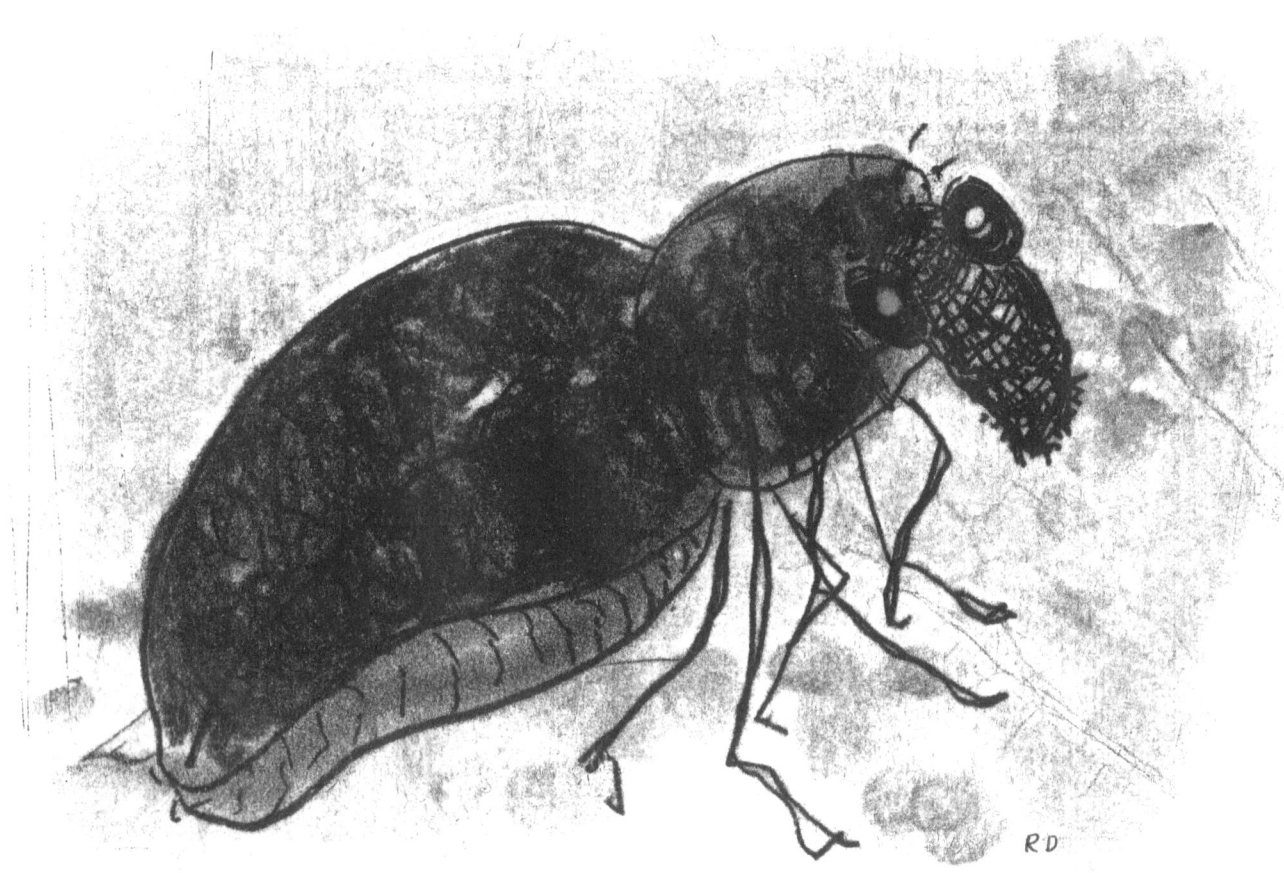

The Jockey

I have won all the prizes
For leaping and vaulting and springing
Over gates, and even over houses.

It is all a matter of concentration –
To know just when
To respond
To the urge
To lift off
In time to the wind's beckoning.

The wind is the horse that bears me.
And I am the jockey.

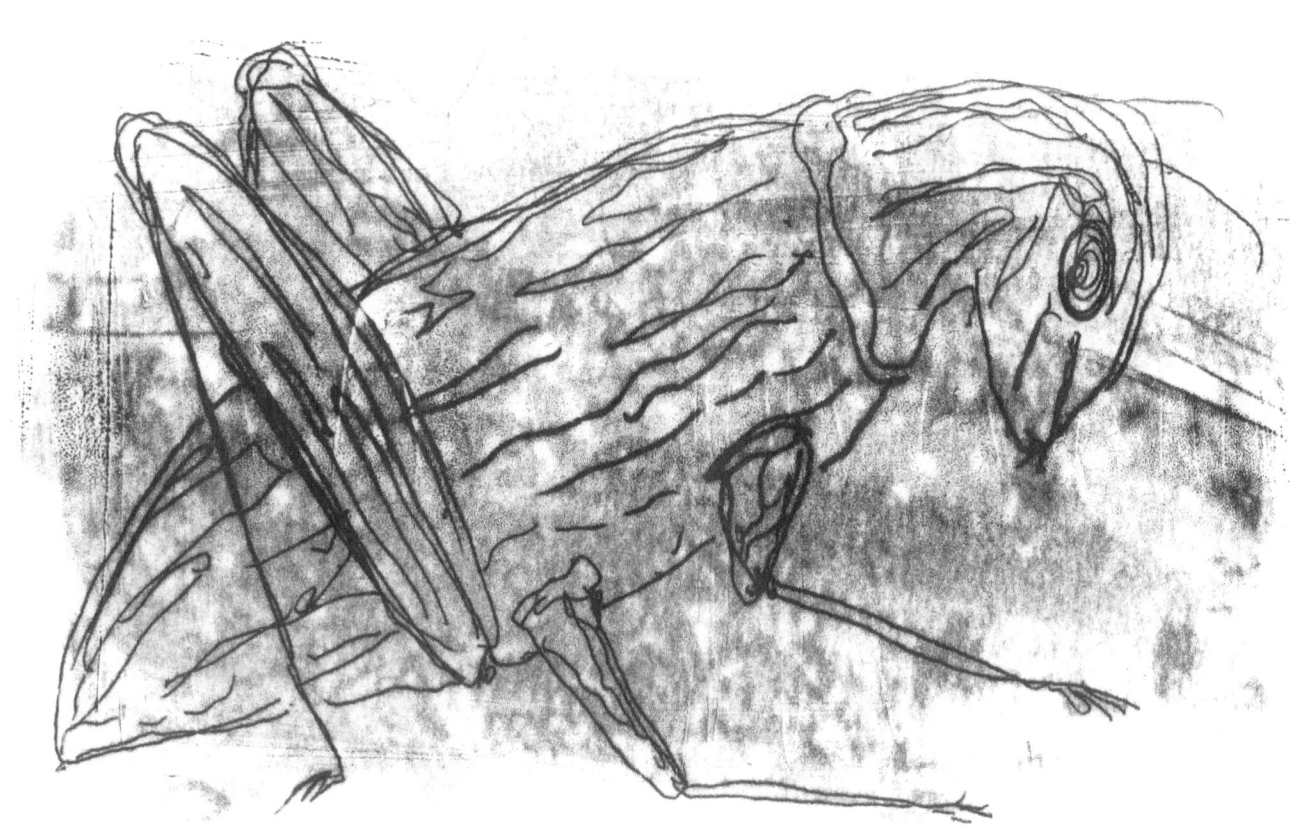

Nectar-thirsters

Oh, we are all so nectar-thirsty!
That is why we have arrived here
In such a hurried, frenzied tangle,
In such a thready, floaty dangle
Of all our bits and pieces...

To strike at the heart of it!
To nuzzle in deep, ever deeper,
With egg on our faces,
To sniff and to taste and to breathe in
All this talcum-powdery sweetness...

Who will win?
Who will get there first?
Who will be the last,
The oh so disappointed?

Calling to the Bees

I am waiting here now.
I am all your pleasure.
I am your day's delight,
And your night's sweet promise.
You can never miss me.

My openness says:
Here I am! Take me!
My colours will dazzle you.
My gentle open lolling will be a ravishment.

I am never not here for you –
Today, that is,
And not forever.
Tomorrow, in my place here,
There will be someone else,
Not unlike me.

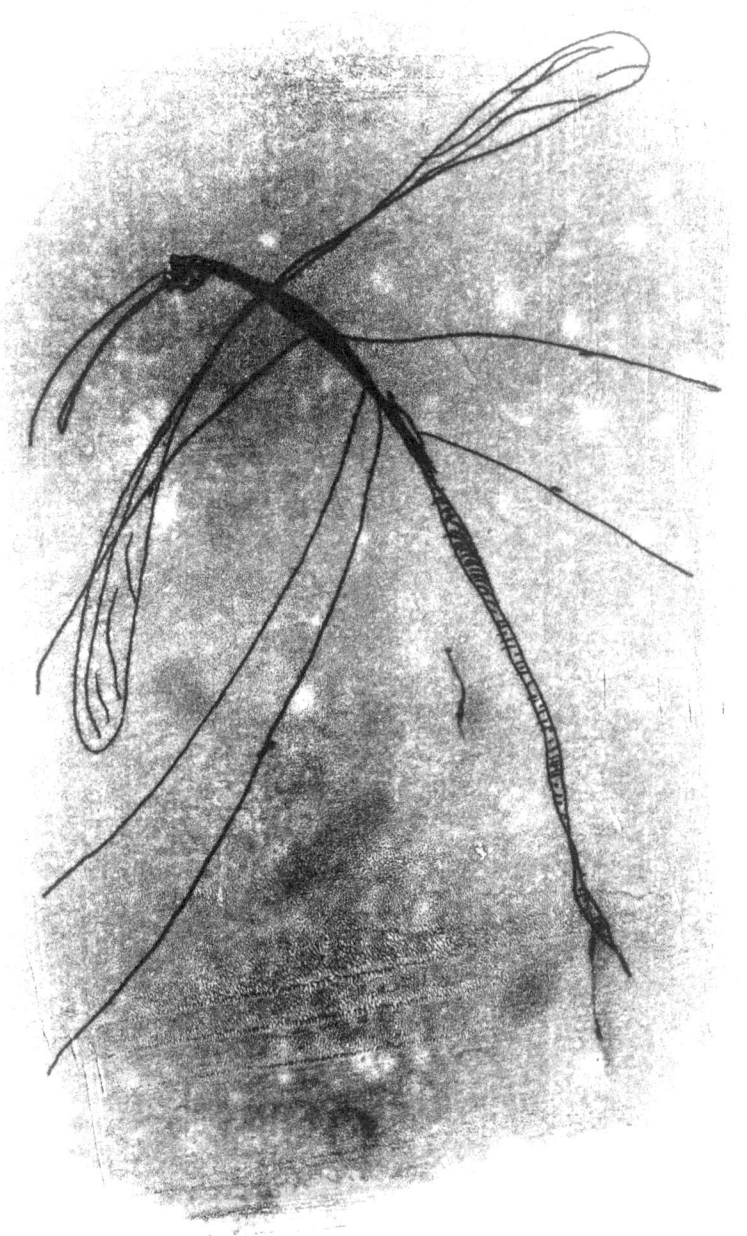

Swimming in the Air

To swim in the air,
Lighter than breath,
Is to dance like this,
Quite lazily,
Between here and nowhere,
With my legs
Gently floating everywhere.

The hours pass so easily,
Morning, noon, evening.
No one has invited me.
Time has no ending.
Close your eyes
And make space for me.

Mighty Leaper

The machinery of my body –
Tense, taut, steady –
Is all tucked and poised and ready
For lift off to the window,

Where I will wait again,
Preparing for the leap that will take me
To that lavender bush
Beside the hedgerow.

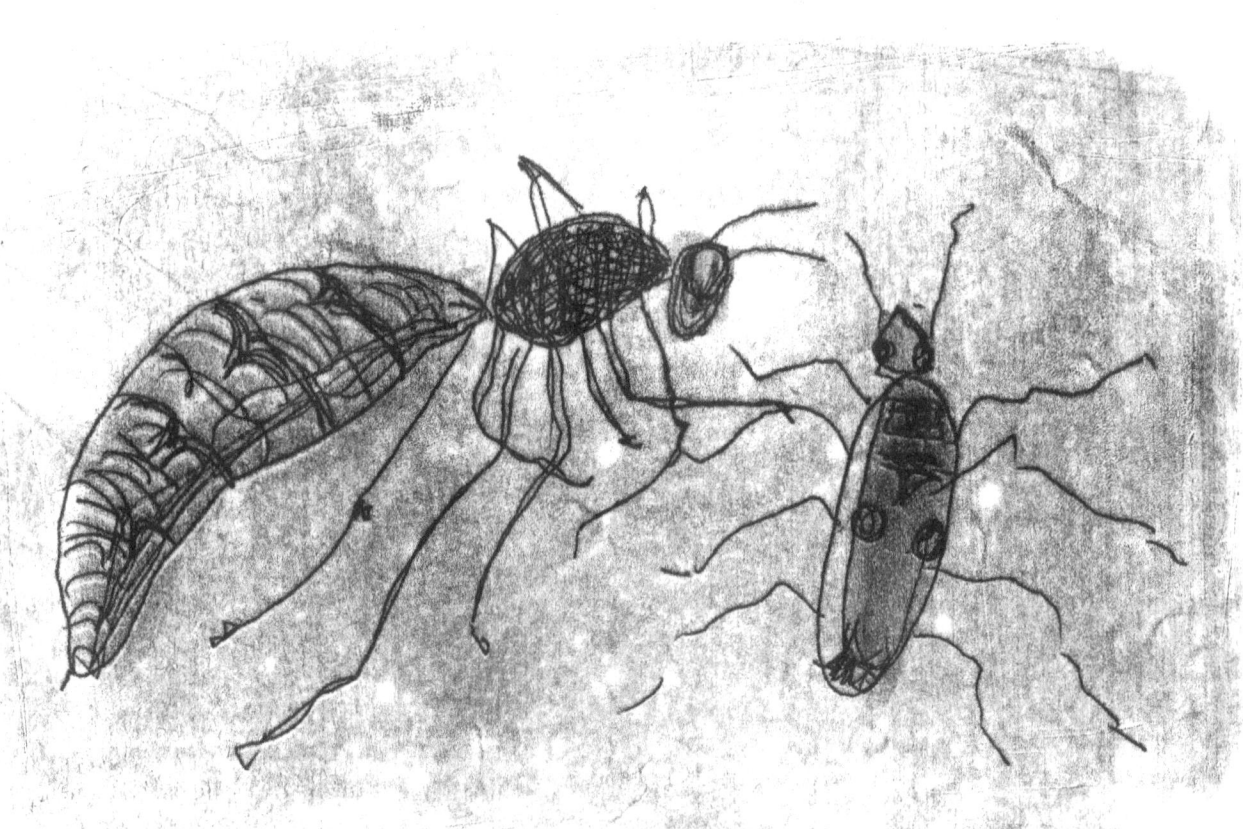

Almost Meeting

Was it love, I ask you?
And did you reply?
We came, we saw, we waited,

Two together,
Lazily suspended,
Not quite touching.
You raised a feeler.
I did likewise.
Then we parted.

Have you remembered,
As I have, that moment?

Lazy Summer Flying

Patience, my little friend,
With your water glass and your biscuit!
Soon enough I will be with you.

But, just for the moment,
A little sky-diving will do,
A slow-turning curve against the wind,

Buoyed up,
And held suspended,
With both wings fanning thinly,

Before I begin the great descent
Towards your table in the garden.

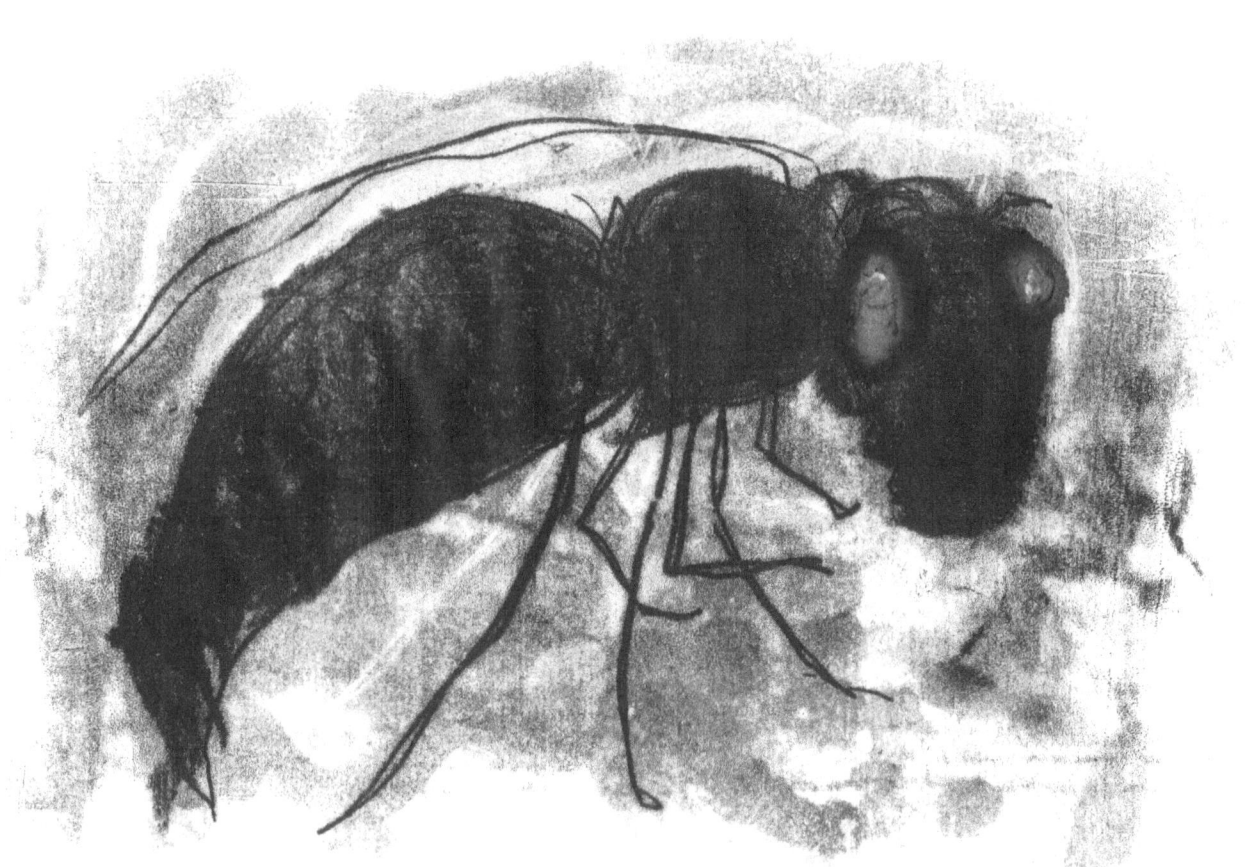

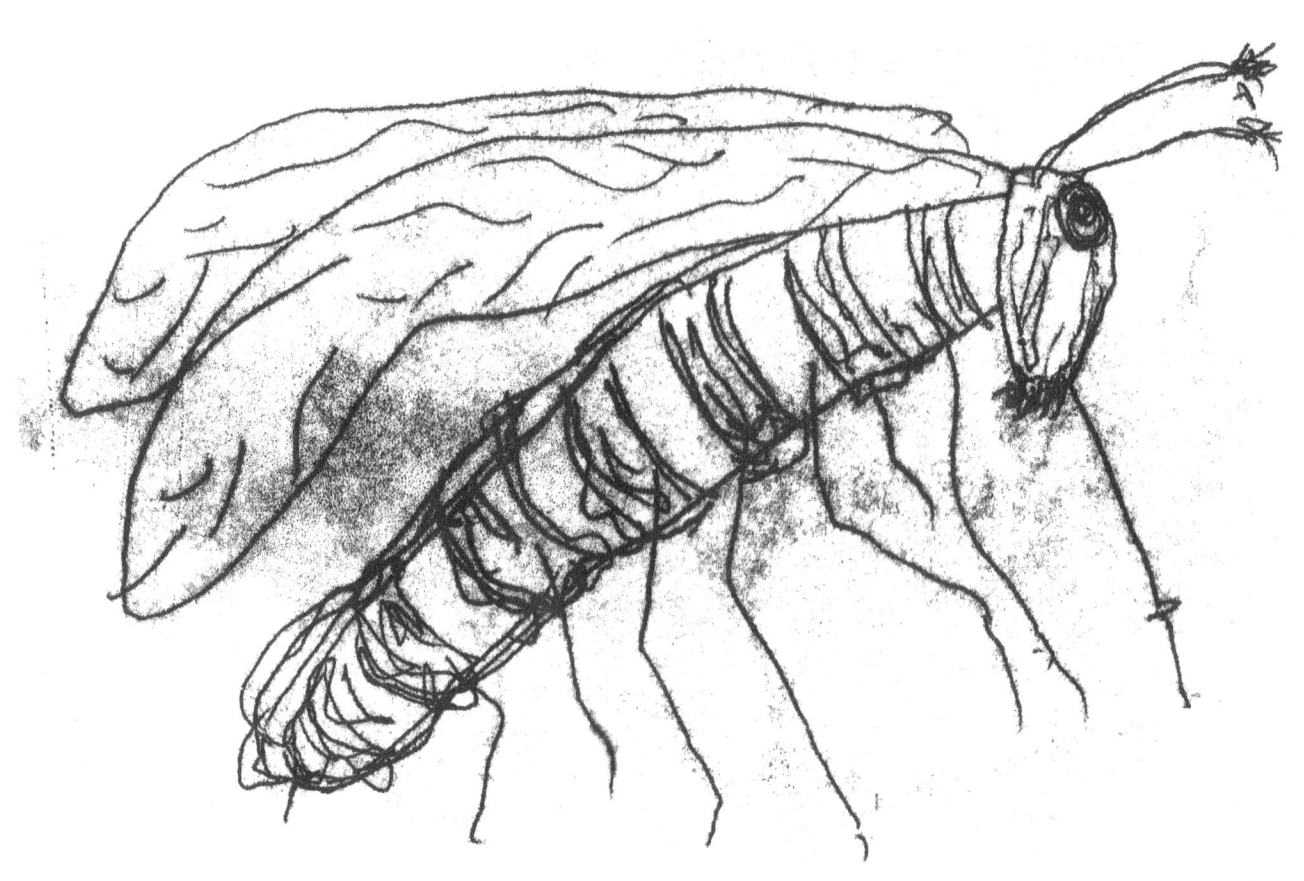

Creeping Around

There is such pleasure to be had
From creeping, climbing, nosing
Behind, amongst, between,
These leaves and these tendrils.

Even when crowded and excited,
We move with caution,
Giving space where space is needed,

Stepping back,
Attending – who wouldn't? I ask you –
To the small delights of
Crispness, smoothness, wetness,
Smells and gentle swaying...

Summer Trumpet

All summer I have prepared myself for this
Unfurling trumpet still in the making
Which opens out to greet you with such flourish.

Come buy my nectar, come buy!
No nonsense,
All is freely given.

Drop in, in passing.
I am that casual about it.

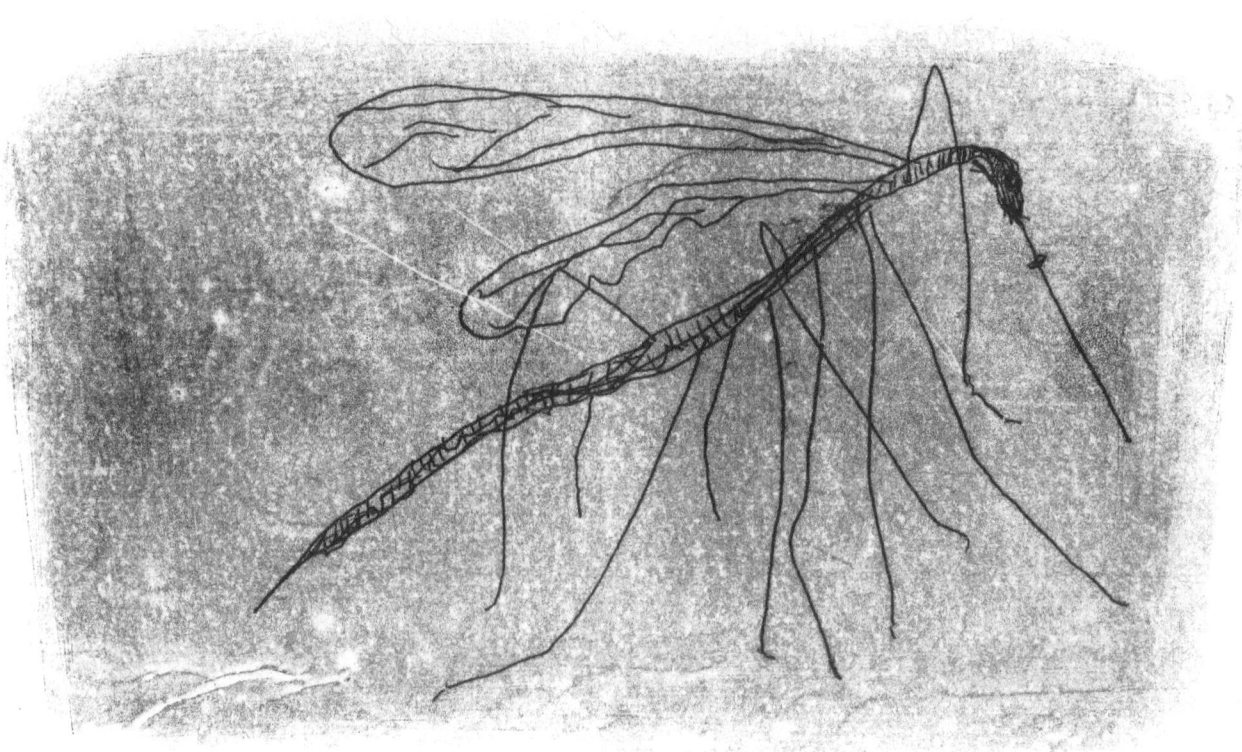

Legs in Disorder

Which leg
Steps out first,
The third one
Or the seventh
Or the fourth?

I am in such a muddle
This morning,
Stuck between this window ledge
And the gate to the garden,
That nothing is happening.

Will these wings help me?
Can you get them disentangled?

The Resting Place

Back here again I come
To this sweet resting place
For creatures such as I am.

No one tells us it is here.
There is no whispered conversation.
We lift off and then we land
As if we knew beforehand.

And that is all there is to be said
About the beauty of this thin lolling limb.
It's just one of those gifts from a sky-blue heaven.

Vintage & Contemporary: Michael Glover and Ruth Dupré

About the artist

Ruth Dupré trained at London's Royal College of Art. She has exhibited in many high profile galleries and museums, including the Whitechapel, the Victoria and Albert, the Barbican, the Royal Academy, and the ICA. She has had several solo shows at ARTHOUSE1, and has work in the collections of the National Portrait Gallery and the Corning Museum of Glass, New York.

She has won the Jack Goldhill Award for Sculpture at the Royal Academy's Summer Exhibition, and has been the joint winner of the Bombay Sapphire Prize for Glass. She has received many other awards from the British Council, Film London and the Crafts Council. Her work has been included in many publications.

www.ruthdupre.co.uk
Instagram: ruth_dupre

Other publications by Michael Glover

Poetry:

Measured Lives (1994)
Impossible Horizons (1995)
A Small Modicum of Folly (1997)
The Bead-Eyed Man (1999)
Amidst All This Debris (2001)
For the Sheer Hell of Living (2008)
Only So Much (2011)
Hypothetical May Morning (2018)
Messages to Federico (2018)
What You Do With Days (2019)
One Season in Hell (2020)

Others:

Headlong into Pennilessness (2011)
Great Works: Encounters with Art (2016)
Playing Out in the Wireless Days (2017)
111 Places in Sheffield You Should Not Miss (2017)
Late Days (2018)
Neo Rauch (2019)
The Book of Extremities (2019)
Thrust (2019)
John Ruskin: an idiosyncratic dictionary (2019)
Rose Wylie (2020)
Whose? (2020)
The Trapper (2021)

As editor or contributor:

Memories of Duveen Brothers (1976)
Goin' down, down, down: Matthew Ronay (2006)
Between Eagles and Pioneers: Georg Baselitz (2011)
Robert Therrien (2016)
Monique Frydman (2017)